Back To Gold

Title: Back To Gold
Genre: Non-Fiction
Desc: Learn the history of gold from ancient to modern times and learn why this precious metal has influenced every facet of our lives.
Author: Kambiz Mostofizadeh
Publisher: Mikazuki Publishing House
ISBN-13: 978-1942825098
Date Published: July 2016

Disclaimer: Information in this book SHOULD NOT be construed to be Investment Advice. Investment Advice should only be sought from a licensed professional.

Back To Gold

TABLE OF CONTENTS

Back To Gold

GOLD IS FROM SPACE

Nearly 4 billion years ago the earth was bombarded for a long period of time with meteorites. These meteorites left holes in the earth not unlike the craters on the Moon. It is believed that the Moon may have been a piece of a (star) or planet that collided with earth, forming the earth as it currently is, before bouncing off and being trapped in the earth's rotation. The meteorites that crashed in to earth brought rare precious metals with them such as Gold. According to NASA, a 3 meter sized asteroid crashed over the Sierra Nevada mountains (near Sutter's Mill where the 1848 Gold Rush began) weighing approximately 50,000 Kilograms. 50,000 Kilograms of an asteroid could be potentially equivalent to 1,760,000 ounces in precious metals. It was this asteroid that is believed to have provided the Gold found at Sutter's Mill sparking the great California Gold Rush. Because the earth's surface was for the most part covered

Back To Gold

in water, the oceans of the earth contain the largest amount of Gold and precious metals. Gold is precious because it arrived on Earth 4 billion years ago from Space, making it rare and valuable. The world's oceans are said to contain one hundred and fifty thousand tons or more of Gold and possibly even larger amounts of other precious metals. The amount of Gold on earth is limited to the means available to produce it. It is

Gold In Earth's Crust	
Type	Parts Per Million
Sedimentary rocks	.0051
Folded belt region	.0038
Crystalline rocks	0036
Continental crust	.0035
Oceanic crust	.0035
Earth's crust	.0035
Continental shield region	.0034
Sub oceanic region	.0029
Deep oceanic region	.004

Source: Tung and Chi-Lung

thought that the entire crust and even the core of the earth, contains vast amounts of untapped Gold waiting to be discovered. Gold

Back To Gold

is an important component in the earth's creation and it is possible that there are molten rivers of Gold far below the earth's crust whose discovery is prevented by our lack of technology. Gold's rarity is because Gold is not a naturally grown commodity like an orange is. Gold was delivered to Earth by space meteorites and it only happened 4 billion years ago. Gold cannot be cloned like plants and even animals can. Gold cannot create more Gold, as the alchemists in the Middle Ages lead potentates to believe. Do you remember the last time you witnessed extended periods of time of space meteorites crashing in to earth delivering you money in the form of precious metals? Neither do I. Gold was sent from Space making it very rare and valuable, unlike fruits and nuts. Saffron may be one of the most expensive spices to purchase but it can be re-planted and re-grown. Gold cannot be reproduced or manufactured from anything but

Back To Gold

Gold. Looking at the chart by Tung and Chi-Lung (page 4), the deep oceanic region contains the least Parts Per Million (PPM) but due to the vastness of the world's oceans comprising the majority of the earth, there may be a lack of testing to determine indeed how much the deep oceanic crust contains. From a geological point of view, it is important to note that the entire earth was at one point covered in water.

Back To Gold

HISTORY OF GOLD

Joshua passing River Jordan with Ark of the Covenant

According to the BBC (Sep 2011), nearly 4 Billion years ago a meteorite shower blasted gold in to the earth's crust creating large craters like those seen on the moon. According to legend, the Ark of the Covenant that contained the Ten Commandments was said to be made of wood gilded in Gold with solid gold plates on the inside and outside. The top of the Ark was also made of solid gold and the cherubim or winged angels were carved gold.

Back To Gold

The artisans and craftsmanship used in the creation of the Ark of the Covenant was more than likely done by Egyptian skilled gold artisans. Egyptians mastered the art of copper craftsmanship and they were known to gild the sarcophagus of important persons in gold. The handles connected to the chest which enabled 4 men to carry the Ark of the Covenant were also made of solid gold. The amount of Gold that was used in the Ark is unknown as efforts are still being made to attempt to locate it. Some scholars believe that the Ark of the Covenant contained up to 75 kilos or more of Gold. The Gold required to build the Ark, was donated by the people, and was melted down to be used by the artisans, in the creation of this timeless masterpiece of craftsmanship. In around 500 B.C.E. King Darius I of the Persian Empire introduced gold coins, following the standard that was set previously by the King of Lydia in modern day western

Back To Gold

dem Volck/vnd sprach: Jr solt kein Feldgeschrey machen/noch ewer stimme hören las-
sen/noch ein Wort auß ewerem Mund geben/biß auff den Tag/wenn ich zu euch sa-
gen werde: Macht ein Feldgeschrey/so macht denn ein Feldgeschrey.

3 Also gieng die Lade deß Herren rings vmb die Statt einmal/vnd kamen in das
Lager/vnd blieben drinnen/Den Josua pflegt sich deß Morgens frü auffzumachen/
vnd die Priester trugen die Lade deß Herren: So trugen die sieben Priester die sieben Halljars Posaunen für der Lade deß Herren her/vnd giengen vnd bliesen Po-
saunen/

Woodcut of the Ark of the Covenant (1640-1660 A.D)

Turkey. Gold is, according to the Oxford
University Press, "a yellow precious metal, the
chemical element of atomic number 79, valued
especially for use in jewelry and decoration,
and to guarantee the value of currencies." The
popularity of gold is seen far and wide from
Ireland, who has the Leprechaun guarding a
pot of gold at the end of the rainbow to King
Midas of Ancient Greece who had the
unfortunate (or fortunate) gift of turning in to

Back To Gold

Achaemenid Daric Gold Coin

gold everything that he touched. In ancient times, Gold had many other uses, not just limited to currency and jewelry. In the tomb of Beni Hassan, Egyptian hieroglyphics show the extraction and refining of gold.

Many Egyptian rulers had their bodies wrapped in Gold in ritual form upon their death. Gold artists in Egypt and Arabia probably obtained

Back To Gold

their supplies from Persia and India. According to the Superfund Research Program by Dartmouth University, Egyptians learned and improved on smelting methods of copper used by Persia (also known as Mesopotamia). Because gold is soft and malleable, it must be mixed with another to harden it to the point that it could be used for jewelry and ornamental purposes. The ancient Chinese also used gold in the creation of sculptures of their deities. According to Homer, The Temple of Solomon was gilded with gold. In the Greek epic Iliad, there are references to gold being woven in to clothing and textiles. In 64 B.C.E., the Emperor Nero re-built his golden from gold that he had plundered from all the areas in Italy, with the purpose of melting the gold to be gilded on his new edifice. The Anglo-Saxons and Danish also incorporated this in to their royal designs in the 10th and 11th century. The Knights Templars, which were the strongest and richest

Back To Gold

military organization in the Christian world, grew in power because of their control of European Gold. The gold which the Knights Templars held belonged to various Kings and Queens and royalty of Europe. The Knights Templars acted as the banking system in Europe during the Middle Ages and became rich from lending gold to fund the operations of various Kings and Queens. The Knights Templars became the largest land owning organization in Europe, if not the world, at that time. Their almost total control on gold and banking, drew the sharp wrath of Pope Clement V and King Phillip IV, who in turned persecuted them to receive their gold (and to wipe away any remaining debt). The gold banking system of the Knights Templars was so advanced that if you gave them gold at one of their Temples (Banks) in France, you would receive a slip of paper (a cheque) which when presented at another of their Temples would

Back To Gold

result in you receiving your money. The Chinese referred to this as Flying Money and the ancient Persian Empire systematized this form of transaction through the creation of the cheque system. King Edward I was also wrapped in a cloth of gold before being buried. In the 13th Century, residents of Bangkok gave their gold to the city to be melted in to one 5.5 ton Gold Buddha (known as Wat Traimit) statue that would be too heavy to steal by foreign invaders of Thailand. Venice played a major part in the 15th century in the manufacture of Gold and Venetian gold was seen used extensively to decorate papal and royal scepters. The Spanish Empire built its power on Gold. The discovery of the New World enabled Spain to reach its pinnacle of power from the vast mineral resources it found in America. The legend of "El Dorado" or the city of gold, drove the Spanish conquistadores to commit horrible atrocities against the Native

Back To Gold

Americans. Whole villages were taken hostage and tortured until information was released as

Knights Templar in traditional battle garb

to the location of El Dorado. El Dorado, was nothing more than a myth, but that did not stop the Spanish from searching for it. Vast amounts of Gold was shipped in the Atlantic

Back To Gold

Ocean and in the Mediterranean. English privateers sought to capture or destroy Spanish shipping lines during the economic rivalry for world domination. Many Spanish ships containing Gold and other valuable metals, sank to the bottom of the Atlantic Ocean and the Mediterranean. On July 20th, 1985, treasure hunter Mel Fischer, after 20 years of searching, discovered sunken Spanish galleon Nuestra Señora de Atocha with the help of archeologist Duncan Matthewson. The Atocha had sunk in 1622 off the Florida Keys and contained vast amounts of treasure. Fischer was able to only locate half of the treasure contained in the Atocha. That half which he discovered contained 40 tons of Gold, over one hundred thousand gold and silver coins, artifacts, and silver ingots worth over four hundred million US dollars. Odyssey, a Florida based salvage company had discovered a sunken Spanish warship by the

Back To Gold

name of Nuestra Señora de Las Mercedes off the coast of Portugal and Spain. Over five hundred thousand gold and silver coins worth four hundred and fifty million US dollars were discovered, but were returned to the Spanish Government, due to their nature of being historical artifacts.

"I reached my hand down and picked it up; it made my heart thump, for I was certain it was gold." - James Marshall, 1848

Prospectus for Australian gold mine

Back To Gold

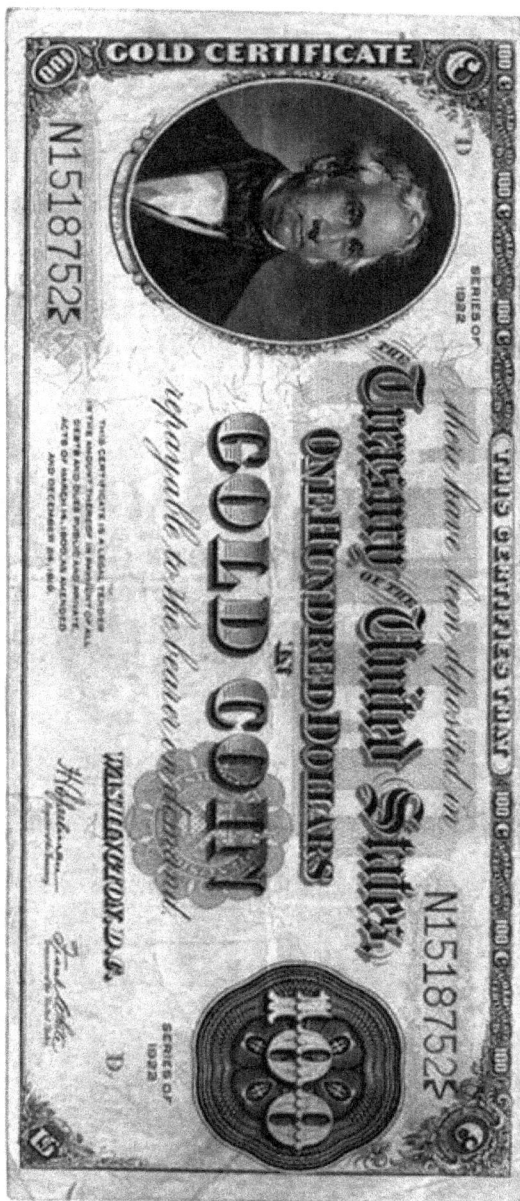

Back To Gold

CAGLIOSTRO

Cagliostro is the most famous con-artist and charlatan to have ever lived. Born in Palermo, Italy in 1743, Cagliostro's real name was Joseph Balsamo. He lost his father at a young age and was sent to a monastery for education at age 15. When he became of age, Cagliostro joined an organized crime group that specialized in financial fraud and was a leading white collar con-man among his peers. For the various financial crimes he committed, he was arrested and spent time in the prison of Palermo. During this time, he had acquired the reputation of being an alchemist or a person that can change base metals in to gold. Using this reputation Cagliostro was able to trick a silversmith named Marano out of 60 ounces of gold. Marano soon realized that he had been conned and issued a death threat to Cagliostro. Cagliostro fled Europe for the

Back To Gold

Cagliostro

Back To Gold

Middle East, settling in the city of Medina, where he became an apprentice of another supposed Greek alchemist named Altotas. From Medina, they travelled to Alexandria, Egypt and sold a large amount of flax that they profited greatly from. Next they travelled to Turkey where they sold all curing drugs and magical amulets. After a brief stay in Malta, Cagliostro left for Rome, where he became famous for selling his elixir vitae. This elixir was supposed to cure all illnesses and extend the life of its drinker. It was here that he met and married Lorenza Feliciana, a young lady from a poor but noble family. He taught her the ways of charlatanry so that she could assist him in his endeavors. After the marriage, they visited Cagliostro's mentor the Count de St. Germain. With his support, the Cagliostros embarked on a European tour, mostly Russia, Poland, and Germany, selling their all-curing Elixir Vitae to

Back To Gold

whomever they could convince of its magical properties. In July 1776, they arrived in London, England with 3000 English Pounds. He quickly setup operations, putting out the word that he alone held the secret to the Philosophers Stone or the secret to change base metals in to gold. Cagliostro's popularity grew rapidly in London and his home was always filled with eager fans. But instead of conning the Londoners, he himself was conned out of nearly 1000 English Pounds (a very huge sum in 1776) by a Lord Scot and Lady Scot that claimed to be Scottish nobility and promised to introduce Cagliostro to all the important families in England. The Scots turned out to be an organized gang preying on victims like Cagliostro. From being arrested on false charges to being held at gun point by Lord Scot, Cagliostro had had enough of England and left for Brussels, Belgium before 1780. They left with only 50 English Pounds

Back To Gold

American Gold Eagle Coin

from the 3000 they had brought with them to England. In Brussels, the Cagliostros were wildly successful selling their all curing drug named Elixir Vitae, from there they went to Strasbourg, Austria where their reputation had preceded them. They were received with open arms and welcomed by all. Their all curing drug was the talk of the town and people lined up to buy it. Old women bought it to the point of

Back To Gold

hoarding it and the Cagliostros enjoyed their most success yet. Count de Cagliostro went to Paris for two weeks and returned to Strasbourg, hoping to move his home to the countryside.

Upon his return he realized the people were not welcoming him anymore. Now they were hurling curses at him and openly calling him a liar and a charlatan. From there he went on to Bordeaux, France where he experienced the same thing as Strasbourg, initial success followed by contempt. The

Back To Gold

Cagliostros went on to Paris where they had the unfortunate luck of being implicated as sorcerers. Cagliostro was sent to the infamous Bastille prison but was released and told to leave Paris. The Cagliostros arrived in London but their welcome was short and they left for Italy, where Count de Cagliostro was arrested in 1789 on charges on heresy and sorcery. He was to be condemned to death but this was changed to life imprisonment in the Castle of St. Angelo. The many arrests, failures, and mistakes had ruined his health and Cagliostro died in 1790, at the age of 47.

Back To Gold

1848

The Gold Rush in California started when James Marshall in January 24, 1848 discovered Gold nugget while building a sawmill in California. The news of his discovery spread like wildfire and the Gold Rush began, sparking a huge wave of migrants and immigrants to the West looking for Gold. Over 140,000 immigrants crossed in to California with the goal of becoming rich from the discovery of gold. Chinese immigrants went on

Back To Gold

to make up a large portion of the Gold panners working the California Gold mines. 1849 became known as the year of the Gold Rush and entire fortunes were made from a single discovery. The West grew on the strength of the gold discoveries that fueled the construction of local towns which provided the workers for the mines. The city of San Francisco became a powerhouse on the West Coast, solely fueled by the Gold of 1849. The real winners were the landowners, shop-owners, and merchants that raised the prices of their goods and services so much that most of the gold miners were unable to break even causing to leave the industry within a few years. The first persons that worked the land in 1849 in search of Gold were Native Americans, runaway soldiers, anyone that thought they could get rich. On July 7th, 1846 the Annexation of California from Mexico by the United States was announced. In 1848 Gold

Back To Gold

was discovered by U.S. soldiers on Sutter's Fort and by 1849, California was being filled with immigrants and constant arrivals of ships from the East Coast. Black Slaves were among the first to work the Gold Mines in California. Even though California had outlawed slavery, that did not stop Southern slave owners from bringing Slaves to California. And it did not stop bounty hunters looking for runaway slaves from kidnapping slaves and taking them back to the South. After the first year, there were over 100,000 persons working the lands of California in search of Gold. By the 2nd year, the number had dropped due to the low amount of Gold that was being found. Not everyone found Gold and even persons that did find Gold, found that the return was not enough to make it financially feasible. The announcement of Gold was felt by some nations as really an excuse by the Federal Government to populate the West Coast of the

Back To Gold

United States. Over 50,000 Englishman arrived in California but focused more on farming initially before turning to the Gold industry. Australian gold prospector Edward Hargraves got his start on the California gold fields before turning back to Australia. Areas that are geologically similar to California have historically yielded similar amounts or more of Gold. Gold panning is highly inefficient and time consuming for the gold panner. This did not stop people arriving on the West Coast to benefit, even if indirectly, from this newfound immense source of wealth. Many of the inventions in modern America, like Levi's Jeans, come from this era. The gold panners spent so much time with their knees hitting the dirt that their pants would rip easily. Levi Strauss invented denim and opened a shop in Market Street in San Francisco so that the gold panners could work endlessly without having to worry about ripped pants. The gold pan which

Back To Gold

came in to creation during this time is still being used today by modern day gold panners.

Prospectus for Australian Gold Mine

Back To Gold

AUSSIE GOLD

When English naval explorer Captain Cook discovered Australia in 1770, he was unaware of the amount of Gold it held. The Australian Gold Rush started in 1851, when Edward Hargraves discovered fives grain of gold in Lewis Ponds Creek and was appointed Commissioner of Crown Lands for the discovery. In 1852 alone, the amount of gold produced by Australian mines was four million eight hundred and ninety thousand ounces, totaling nearly 20 million English Pounds. The export of Australian Gold was immediately outlawed to possible prevent the gold from reaching England. Hargraves started his gold mining career in the gold mines of California. After having compared the California and Australian rock formations, he concluded that Australia held a vast amount of untapped resources. Many of the early Australian oilfields

Back To Gold

were worked by Chinese immigrant labor. The
discovery of Gold resulted in mass immigration

Chinese immigrant working on gold fields

to Australia and the amount of prisoners in
Australia went up to nearly 2 million persons!
Every store near the active gold mine sold

Back To Gold

items related to gold mining. Robbers began to frequent gold mines and gold fields, to steal away the hard work of the miners. Police corruption became rampant as licenses to gold mines were sold and re-sold to multiple individuals simultaneously. Gold mining also created problems such as the price of homes was so high that the average miner could not afford to own one, social problems created living discomfort, criminal activity was widespread in the gold mining areas, and the rent of homes was beyond the reach of most workers. This resulted in political clashes between gold miners and local authorities, prompting the Australian Government to send troops from Melbourne to crush the revolt. The political leader and engineer Peter Lalor representing the gold miners was elected to the Victorian parliament, where he was able to champion the rights of the gold miners.

Back To Gold

Gold miners in Queensland, Australia

Today, Australia has multiple mines that have over 30 tons of gold within them and scores of gold that has yet not been found. Gold mining is a major industry in today's Australia and many of its more powerful mining companies have expanded internationally to North America, Africa, and Asia.

Back To Gold

GOLD PROSPECTING

Privately minted Gold coin

Central Banks buy gold to add to their reserves as a defense against the volatility of international markets. Up until 1912, the Olympic Games Gold Medal was actually made from pure Gold! Gold, although not known for exceedingly high returns, has historically been a safe investment for banks,

Back To Gold

governments, and even corporations. According to Forbes magazine, the United States is the largest holder of Gold reserves in the world with 8,133.5 tons. It is estimated that there are over 150,000 tons of Gold in the world's oceans. On land, according to BBC, there are 1.3 grams of gold per 1,000 tons of other material in the Earth's crust. It is theorized by scientists that it was during the creation of the earth that gold was sent in to the Earth's crust. It has proven that meteors and other space debris that have crashed in to the earth, have contained gold in them. If you gathered all the mined gold in the world, it would not fill up two Olympic sized swimming pools. According to various leading Gold experts, the remaining minable Gold in the world will run out in 10 to 20 years. According to their prognostications, the remaining gold that is needed to be used for electronics will be recycled gold. In 1932, Gold was $20 USD per

Back To Gold

ounce. As of this writing, Gold is over $1300 USD per ounce.

Un-refined gold

The largest alluvial Gold Nugget discovered was named the Welcome Stranger and it weighed over 71 kilograms. It was discovered in Victoria, Australia by John Deason and Richard Oates on 5 February 1869.

Lode gold is gold that is contained within solid rock. The areas that are most likely to contain valuable lode deposits of gold have already been explored carefully and thoroughly. In the current economic environment, the prospector

Back To Gold

that is lacking in experience and money to fund
operations, will have very little chance of

Gold Panning

Back To Gold

Gold Miner in front of Gold Mine

discovering a lode rich enough to develop. A
placer deposit is a concentration of natural

Back To Gold

material that has accumulated in the unconsolidated sediments of a stream bed. Heaviness and resistance to corrosion make gold an ideal substance to accumulate in placer deposits. Panning is the simplest method of separating the gold from the silt, sand, and gravel of the stream deposits.
It is the method most commonly used by the beginning prospector. The gold pan is an indispensable prospecting tool that is versatile, efficient, inexpensive, and easy to carry.
With some practice, even an inexperienced gold seeker should be able to recover most of the gold from the sand and gravel. Taking a sample of the soil and having it assayed it professionally, will tell you how much gold is in one ton of dirt. Gold is much heavier than the minerals that make up the sand and gravel and when the water is shaken and swirled, the

Back To Gold

grains and flakes of gold sink and collect on the bottom of the pan. The lighter materials are washed away from the gold and removed from the pan.

"The world is changed because you are made of ivory and Gold."
-Oscar Wilde

Back To Gold

The entire process of panning consists of collecting and washing. The panners are using their pans to dig in to the earth (the soil) and once they have collected it, they wash it to remove the lighter materials in the pan to allow the heavier materials which are the gold, to be seen. Gold collected in a creek bed varies and the equipment used also gives advantages. A dredge has enabled some miners to find huge rocks of Gold. A gold pan will allow for the collection of very small nuggets and gold flakes, which when accumulated give you usable gold. A creek that gives you ½ an ounce of Gold per 1 ton of dirt/sand is financially worth working. Anything less than this is not feasible and could result in financial losses for your operation. That is precisely why it is essential for you to have a professional soil sample conducted by a geologist and an assayer to determine if it is financially feasible to purchase the rights to the land or the land

Back To Gold

itself. When you purchase the rights to work the land for Gold (the mineral rights alone), this is known as a Un-Patented Claim. When you purchase the land with the rights to the minerals, this is known as a Patented Claim. The system of Patented and Un-Patented Claims came about to prevent abuses in real estate sales and mineral rights sales. In many cases, the rights to one piece of land were sold multiple times to multiple buyers, causing lawsuits and in some cases violence to occur. When you are a Patented Claim owner of a piece of land, you are the rightful owner in deed and you have the rights to the minerals laying in it. Even if you choose not to work the land for Gold, you can sign a 50/50 deal with an operator to work the land in return for commission. In other words, you are allowing a person or company to find Gold on your land, produce it, and share the profits with you 50/50. Your only cost is purchasing the land.

Back To Gold

The operator will be responsible for all costs related to the production of the Gold. As a Patented Claim owner you are responsible for the yearly property taxes and Bureau of Land Management Fees (if any). As the Patented Claim owner, you are also responsible if any ecologically or environmentally damaging accident were to occur on your property. If you are seeking to purchase Gold bearing land, first you should conduct testing with a Geologist and a Gold Assayer to determine how much Gold each ton of dirt contains. If the results are satisfactory and you decide to purchase the land as a Patented Claim owner, then you should also have in mind the potential operators that you could sign a deal with to work your land for Gold. As it is a Joint Venture 50/50 agreement, you will have to maintain some level of oversight so to prevent any unsafe techniques or methods being used in Gold production that could result in permanent

Back To Gold

environmental damage to the land. Many of the major operators in the field do not purchase land as their business model relies on Joint Venture agreements with land owners. Patented Claim land can be purchased for as little as $30,000 in 2016. Un-Patented Claim mineral rights can be purchased for as little as $8,000. If you are purchasing the land as a Patented Claim, then your first order of business will be to entertain signing a Joint Venture deal with various operators. If you purchase an Un-Patented claim to the mineral rights of a land, you are not responsible for any yearly taxes and fees so you can focus on being an operator on that land. As an operator, you are responsible for putting together a team to produce gold from that land. Let us imagine that your resources are limited and you choose to purchase the rights (Un-Patented) for Placer Mining (creek, river, etc). Your first order would be to know where in that creek (for example)

Back To Gold

has the most amount of Gold. The first place to see would be the areas in which there are turns in the creek. The turns in the creek create a vortex that draw the Gold towards it edges. Opposite sides of the turn will hold some level of Gold, but it is up to the Geologist and Assayer to professionally determine the areas that contain the most. The bedrock has also been known to contain Gold, due to its heavy sinking nature. You could also use the Getty Method of attracting investors. You could purchase the land and put together a team of 3 people besides yourself to invest in the project. You can use the funds from the 3 persons and you will oversee the project by hiring a professional operator to work the claim. All land contains Gold in it but it is a matter of how much Gold is contained within 1 ton of dirt from that land. Taking a sample of the earth (the dirt on that land) will allow you to have a

Back To Gold

professionally prepared report by a Geologist and an Assayer, to back your claim.

According to the United States Geological Survey, "Geologists examine all factors controlling the origin and emplacement of mineral deposits, including those containing gold. Igneous and metamorphic rocks are studied in the field and in the laboratory to gain an understanding of how they came to their present location, how they crystallized to solid rock, and how mineral-bearing solutions formed within them. Studies of rock structures, such as folds, faults, fractures, and joints, and of the effects of heat and pressure on rocks suggest why and where fractures occurred and where veins might be found. Studies of weathering processes and transportation of rock debris by water enable geologists to predict the most likely places for placer deposits to form. The occurrence of gold is not

Back To Gold

capricious; its presence in various rocks and its occurrence under differing environmental conditions follow natural laws. As geologists increase their knowledge of the mineralizing processes, they improve their ability to find gold."

LOOK AT THE U.S. GOLD INDUSTRY
In 2015, domestic gold mine production was estimated to be about 200 tons, 5% less than that in 2014, and the value was estimated to be about $7.6 billion. Gold was produced at fewer than 45 lode mines, at several large placer mines in Alaska, and numerous smaller placer mines (mostly in Alaska and in the Western States). About 7% of domestic gold was recovered as a byproduct of processing domestic base-metal ores, chiefly copper. The top 29 operations yielded more than 99% of the mined gold produced in the United States. Commercial-grade gold was produced at about 25 refineries.
Source: U.S. Geological Survey Mineral Commodity Summaries, January 2016

Back To Gold

The content of recoverable free gold in placer deposits is determined by the free gold assay method, which involves amalgamation of gold-bearing concentrate collected by dredging, hydraulic mining, or other placer mining operations. In the period when the price of gold was fixed, the common practice was to report assay results as the value of gold (in cents or dollars) contained in a cubic yard of material. Now results are reported as grams per cubic yard or grams per cubic meter.

"May everything you touch turn to gold."
-Kambiz Mostofizadeh

Back To Gold

PANNING ON FEDERAL LAND

The general rules to be followed when panning for Gold on Federal land is:

    a. Do not build anything on Federal land; no structures, etc.

    b. Do not use machinery of any kind.

    c. Follow the rules of the National Forest or area you are working in.

    d. Do not destroy the stream bed by digging it up.

    e. Use tools that are non-destructive to the environment. A simple Gold pan is an easy tool for gold discovery.

    f. Do not disturb the natural habitat in which you are panning in.

Back To Gold

THE PROCESS

- **Site Preparation**

- **Gold Extraction**
  - a. Pan
  - b. Dredge
  - c. Rocker
  - d. Long Tom
  - e. Sluice Box
  - f. Hydraulic Mining
  - g. Lode Mining

- **Gold Purification**

- **Gold Production**
- a. Bars
- b. Jewelry
- c. Coins
- d. Electronics
- e. Medical
- f. Aerospace
- g. Dental

Back To Gold

GOLD CONS

The attractive nature of Gold as an investment has attracted charlatans, con-artists, thieves, and White Collar bandits, to this highly valuable precious metal. Many unknowing merchants were the victim of purchasing Fool's Gold or Pyrite for a high price while being assured that what they were buying was indeed gold. Un-ethical gold mine sellers have too often placed in random areas of their mine, small gold nuggets (or large ones!) to falsely promote the value of their gold mine to potential buyers. According to the Los Angeles Times, in 1988 there were 52 gold related scams being investigated by authorities. When you purchase gold, you should ask some important questions and they are:

- What is the purity of this Gold? Is it 6K, 10K, 14K, 18K, 22K, or 24K?
- How many grams is the gold?

Back To Gold

- Is the gold solid gold? Does the item you are purchasing contain anything in it other than gold?
- Is this gold new or used?
- What is the origin of the Gold? Where was it made?

Karat	Gold	Other Metal
24K	100%	0%
22K	91.60%	8.60%
18K	75%	25%
14K	58.5%	41.5%
10K	41.7%	58.3%
6K	25%	75%

Note: Karat is a gold unit for purity

Questions to Ask Phone Salesperson

1. Where did you get my phone number from?

2. Can you give me a callback number in case you get cut off?

3. How did you get my name?

4. What is your Manager's Name?

5. Is your business licensed to sell Gold and with whom?

Back To Gold

THE MIDAS TOUCH

King Midas was the King of Phrygia in the region known as Western Asia. Although he was a rich and powerful potentate, he loved Gold more than anything. He would spend all of his time taking inventory of his gold and laying gold over his body. He loved Gold above everything else. He had one wish above all and that was to be able to create gold from whatever he touched. Dionysus granted King Midas his wish and when Midas went to sleep and woke up, he felt different. First he touched a chair that immediately turned to Gold. Then he picked up an apple to eat that also turned to Gold so he was unable to eat it. Then he saw his friend and when he touched his daughter's arm to greet her and his daughter turned to Gold. Midas realized that his love of Gold was destroying his life and the life of the people whom he cared for. He asked Dionysus to reverse the gift in which he had received. Midas went to the river and washed his hands

Back To Gold

Midas turns his daughter in to Gold

Back To Gold

Midas drawing water to wash away curse

Back To Gold

making the curse known as the "Midas Touch" disappear. From that day on, King Midas took value in what he had in his life and stopped worrying about what he wanted to have. This made him live a more ethical and balanced life, that favored natural living over amassing material possessions. What was originally received as a gift had become a curse. The story of King Midas demonstrates that the love of greed and money is a destructive and negative influence.

Creek bed flowing gold

Back To Gold

MONTEZUMA'S GOLD

The Spanish Conquistadors under Cortez sought to find Montezuma in order to convince him to join Catholicism. Montezuma refused and Cortez used this as an opportunity to take advantage of rivalries within the Aztec Kingdom. Some of the Aztecs believed Cortez to be the deity Quetzalcoatl or the "feathered serpent", and they either paid him reverence or followed his command. Using their advanced European weaponry, the Conquistadors under Cortez robbed the Aztec people and looted a portion of their treasury. But Cortez was not able to escape with the gold because he was ambushed by the Aztecs who killed half of Cortez's men. Montezuma was also killed in the mayhem but the Spanish claim that it was the Aztecs that killed Montezuma, rather than the Spanish. The Spanish came back for the Gold a few months later only to find the Gold had been disappeared. In order to find this

Back To Gold

gold, many people were tortured and slaughtered by the so called more sophisticated Europeans. The gold was never found and neither was the fabled city of gold or El Dorado. The Aztecs referred to Gold in their native Nahuatl language as 'teocuitlatl' or 'Excrement of the Gods.' According to legend and hearsay, Montezuma's gold was taken by 8,000 trusted Aztec warriors to the U.S. for hiding from Cortez and the Spanish. It is believed by some gold explorers that the gold of Montezuma that is worth 3 Billion Dollars or more, is hidden somewhere in Utah. According to the legend, the Aztec warriors hid the gold and then killed each other so that their spirits would protect the gold in the afterlife. The current location that the gold is believed to be held is in Kanab, Utah.

"All that glitters is not gold."
-William Shakespeare

Back To Gold

THE TOP 20 GOLD RESERVE HOLDERS

	Nation	Tons	% of Reserves**
1	United States	8,133.5	74.6%
2	Germany	3,380.2	67.9%
3	IMF	2,814.0	n/a
4	Italy	2,451.8	67.6%
5	France	2,435.6	62.7%
6	China	1,808.3	2.1%
7	Russia	1,481.4	14.9%
8	Switzerland	1,040.0	6.2%
9	Japan	765.2	2.4%
10	Netherlands	612.5	61.2%
11	India	557.8	5.9%
12	ECB	504.8	26.4%
13	Turkey	464.1	15.6%
14	Taiwan	422.7	3.7%
15	Portugal	382.5	71.0%
16	Saudi Arabia	322.9	2.1%
17	UK	310.3	8.7%
18	Lebanon	286.8	22.4%
19	Spain	281.6	19.3%
20	Austria	280.0	42.7%

Source: World Gold Council

"Money makes the man, no one who is poor is either good or honored."
- Aristodemus

Back To Gold

RENTING OUT GOLD

The largest Gold Bar in the world, according to Guinness Book of World Records, is 250 kilograms and is displayed at the Toi Gold Museum in Japan. This unique 24K Gold bar was manufactured by the Mitsubishi Materials Corporation of Japan and has appreciated since many times since its creation. According to a Mitsubishi Materials Corporation spokesperson interview with The Japan Times, the Gold Bar is worth 400 million yen and measures 45.5 cm by 22.5 cm at the base and is 17 cm high, According to the World Gold Council, households in Turkey (the 4th largest market globally) have a combined amount of 3,500 tons of "under the pillow" Gold. China is, as of 2016, the number one producer and consumer of Gold in the world. Gold is an asset and in many nations on earth, such as India, you can take your gold jewelry in to a bank and be paid interest on your gold. Some

Back To Gold

Source: Toi Mine

banks pay up to 2 percent or more, depending on the length in which you deposit the gold. You are in effect monetizing un-used gold that is lying in your dresser drawer and receiving

Back To Gold

interest for having deposited in the bank. Once the period in which you have deposited the gold finishes, you are free to take your gold. You made money off gold that was not being used and your gold appreciated making you money from both. It is a win-win situation. The economy wins because the gold that you had hidden in your drawer can now be used in various industries and you win because you will be receiving money from what was just previously trapped capital. Money that is invested but is not giving you returns is considered "trapped capital". It is trapped capital because the money is essentially tied up in a fruitless venture. Gold that is not making you money is trapped capital. By "renting" out your gold to a bank or even to a jeweler, you can receive income from that Gold. The more gold you amass and "rent", the more money you will make.

Back To Gold

Gold Throne of King Tut of Egypt

WASTE

Most of the electronics you have contain Gold in them including your computer and mobile phones. Countless individuals throw away old mobile phones without taking the gold that is in them. According to the Environmental Protection Agency, for every 1 million mobile phones thrown away, there are almost 75 pounds of Gold contained within them. Electronic waste such as second-hand or used

Back To Gold

mobile phone SIM cards contain a small amount of Gold on them. If you removed the Gold off of 70 mobile phone SIM cards, you would probably have something like 1/10th of 1 gram of Gold. The Karat might be between 10K and 14K. Hydro-metallurgy is being used to process kilos of electronic waste for gold extraction. In 20 years or so, when all the minable gold will have been depleted, the most likely source for Gold will be recycled Gold. The current mining costs per ounce of Gold in a mining operation on land is $900. That means $900 USD is spent for every 1 ounce of Gold that is produced in a mining operation. If hydro-metallurgic methods of efficiency are used to extract Gold from electronics in bulk quantities, the price of extracting ounce of Gold will be reduced substantially.

Back To Gold

IN CONTRAST TO REAL ESTATE

Let's take the example of a 2 bedroom 2 bathroom apartment that is 97 square meters in a guard gated complex in Las Vegas. This apartment was sold for $147,000 in 2006, according to public records listed on the website Zillow. As of this writing, the same apartment is listed for $54,000. That means if you would have bought this apartment in 2006 as an investment, after 10 years your money would have lost nearly 2/3rd of its value! <u>You would have lost $100,000 if you had purchased this apartment as an investment.</u> Had you purchased $147,000 worth of Gold as an investment in 2006 at $635 an ounce and sold it today in 2016 at $1300 an ounce, your money would have more than doubled. Your $147,000 would be worth more than $300,000. Gold has, in the opinion of most Gold industry experts, outperformed the real estate in the past ten years (2006-2016).

Back To Gold

GOLD/HOUSING RATIO

The Gold/Housing Ratio is the amount of Gold ounces it would take to purchase one house. To arrive at the Gold/Housing Ratio you must take the National Average Price for a Home and Divide it by the Price of Gold per Ounce.

FORMULA

Average Home Price / Gold Price Per Ounce = Amount of Gold ounces you need to purchase a home

Back To Gold

EXAMPLE

2016 National Median Home Price is $239,700

2016 Gold Price $1,300 an ounce

= 184 Ounces of Gold to Buy a Home

The Past

2001 = 520 Gold Ounces

2016 = 184 Gold Ounces

"Money is the life and soul of mortal men.

He who has not heaped up riches for himself,

wanders like a dead man amongst the living."

-Timocles

South African Gold Miners

Back To Gold

SOUTH AFRICAN GOLD

Forty percent of the Gold that has ever been mined in the world comes from South Africa. Over 1 Billion Ounces of Gold have come out of South Africa since its discovery in 1885. George Walker and George Harrison were the first to discover Gold on an old farm close to Johannesburg, South Africa. They sold their stake for a small amount unknowing that it contained one of the world's greatest sources of wealth.

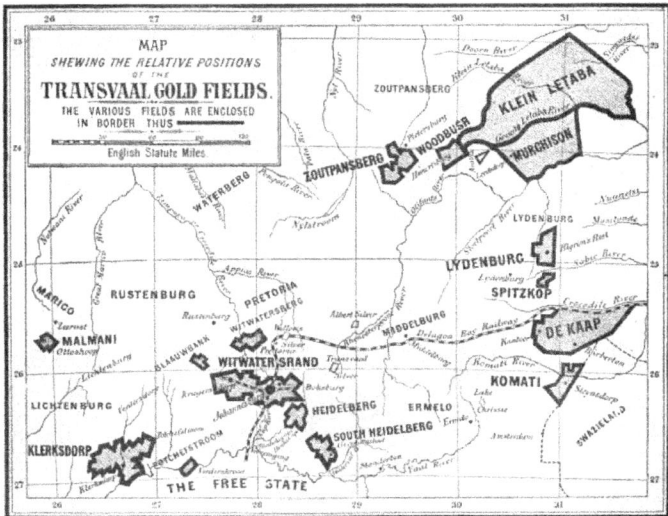

Transvaal Gold Fields

Back To Gold

According to the Scientific Research Society, "the Witwatersrand basin, which covers an area about the size of West Virginia, contains almost as much gold as the rest of the Earth's surface combined." The Witwatersrand Basin was created when a gigantic meteor slammed in to the earth, creating an enormous crater 300 kilometers in height. The impact created so much heat that rocks impacted were melted instantly in to the crust of the earth. The majority of the gold miners are

Back To Gold

Black South Africans and the repeated abuses carried out against them prompted Nelson Mandela to ask miners to stop working the mines if they ever want to achieve equality. The conditions were dangerous but the amount

Back To Gold

of Gold it brought in made the city of Johannesburg and many other cities flourish.

GOLD AS AN INVESTMENT

The best way to purchase Gold as an investment is to do it in the manner that Banks do it and that is purchase Gold Bars. Gold Bars come in various shapes, sizes, and weights, but their being bought in droves by Central Banks proves that they are a viable method for protecting and growing assets. China is the number one consumer of Gold in the world and the amount of Gold they purchase is set to grow greatly as more individuals in their nation come out of poverty. India is also a major consumer of Gold and their markets are also set to grow as incomes begin to rise. Under the pillow Gold has been viewed in traditional cultures as a safe investment and nest egg that has the ability to counteract un-certain economic cycles.

Back To Gold

Back To Gold

Back To Gold

THE GOLD STANDARD

1792	U.S. Congress established Mint
1791-1811	First Bank of the United States
1816-1836	Second Bank of the United States
1861	U.S. Treasury issues Paper Money
1879	Civil War Greenbacks redeemed
1914	Federal Reserve Bank established
1934	Private Gold ownership banned
1944	Breton Woods modified Gold Standard
1971	U.S. abandons Gold Standard
1975	Congress restores private Gold ownership

Source: National Center for Policy Analysis

For 41 years (1934-1975), it was illegal to own Gold in the United States as an investment. In 1971, when the United States officially abandoned the Gold Standard, the Gold Standard has ceased being used for at least 30 years by many nations including England.

Back To Gold

U.S. Treasury Timeline

March 14, 1900	The Gold Standard Act officially placed the United States on the gold standard.
March 6, 1933	President Roosevelt declared a four day national bank holiday to prevent anyone from exporting or hoarding gold or silver
April 5, 1933	President Franklin Roosevelt issued an order making it illegal to hoard gold coin, gold bullion or gold certificates. Violation of this order was punishable by a $10,000 fine or 10 years in prison, making it a felony to own gold. Eventually, gold coins from 1933 and earlier were exempted from this rule so coin collectors could avoid prosecution.
June 5, 1933	The United States abandoned the gold standard. All existing contracts and currency that required redemption in gold were no longer considered valid.
August 28, 1933	President Roosevelt issued Executive Order 6260, which regulated the hoarding and exporting of gold in the United States.
December 28, 1933	President Roosevelt issued Executive Order 6102, ordering anyone who still held gold certificates or gold coins of non-numismatic value to deliver them to the Treasurer of the United States.
January 17, 1934	It became illegal for private citizens to own gold certificates following the implementation of the Gold Reserve Act of 1934.
January 30, 1934	The Gold Reserve Act withdrew gold coins from circulation, provided for the devaluation of the dollar's gold content, and created the Exchange Stabilization Fund.
January 13, 1937	The first deposit of gold bullion was shipped to the United States Bullion Depository at Fort Knox.
April 24, 1964	Secretary C. Douglas Dillon removed the restrictions on acquiring or holding gold certificates.
Continued on the next page	

Back To Gold

U.S. Treasury Timeline

April 26, 1969	Pre-1934 gold coins could be imported into the country and traded without a license from the Department of the Treasury for the first time since 1933. The Treasury decided that preventing the import of pre-1934 gold coins while allowing the same coins to be traded freely domestically was inconsistent and unfair.
December 18, 1971	President Nixon declared that the official U.S. price of gold would be raised to $38 per ounce, devaluing the dollar.
April 3, 1972	President Richard Nixon raised the official U.S. gold price from $35 an ounce to $38 an ounce. The change in gold price was the first made since an Executive Order by President Roosevelt in 1934.
September 23, 1974	An inspection to verify the gold holdings at the Fort Knox Bullion Depository was completed by members of Congress. The inspection was setup in response to conspiracy theories that Fort Knox held little or no gold at all.
December 31, 1974	Ford lifts the 40-year ban, enacted in 1933, on gold ownership by U.S. citizens.

Source: United States Treasury (Treasury.gov)

The exchange rates under an International Gold Standard are pegged to the price of Gold itself. So for example, if Gold was $50 an ounce in America and 5 English Pounds an ounce in England, the exchange rate would be $10 per English Pound.

Back To Gold

South African Gold Field Maps & Concessions (1888)

Back To Gold

FORT KNOX

A large amount of the United States' gold reserves is stored in the vault of the Fort Knox Bullion Depository, one of the institutions under the supervision of the Director of the United States Mint. The remaining gold reserves are held in the Philadelphia Mint, the Denver Mint, the West Point Bullion Depository and the San Francisco Assay Office, also facilities of the United States Mint. The Depository was completed in December 1936 at a cost of $560,000. It is located approximately 30 miles southwest of Louisville, Kentucky, on a site which was formerly a part of the Fort Knox military reservation. The first gold was moved to the Depository by railroad in January 1937. That series of shipments was completed in June 1937. The two-story basement and attic building is constructed of granite, steel and concrete. Its exterior dimensions measure 105 feet by 121 feet. Its height is 42 feet above ground level. The building's construction was

Back To Gold

supervised by the Procurement Division of the Treasury Department, now the Public Buildings Administration of the General Services Administration. Upon its completion, the Depository was placed under the jurisdiction of the Director of the United States Mint.

Within the building is a two level steel and concrete vault that is divided into compartments. The vault door weighs more than 20 tons. No one person is entrusted with the combination. Various members of the Depository staff must dial separate combinations known only to them. The vault casing is constructed of steel plates, steel I-beams and steel cylinders laced with hoop bands and encased in concrete. The vault roof is of similar construction and is independent of the Depository roof. Between the corridors encircling the vault and the outer wall of the building is space used for offices and storerooms. The outer wall of the Depository is

Back To Gold

constructed of granite lined with concrete. Construction materials used on the building included 16,500 cubic feet of granite, 4,200 cubic yards of concrete, 750 tons of reinforcing steel and 670 tons of structural steel. Over the marble entrance at the front of the building is the inscription "United States Depository" with the seal of the Department of the Treasury in gold. Offices of the Officer in Charge and the Captain of the Guard open upon the entrance lobby. At the rear of the building is another entrance used for receiving bullion and supplies. At each corner of the structure on the outside, but connected with it, are four guard boxes. Sentry boxes, similar to the guard boxes at the corners of the Depository, are located at the entrance gate. A driveway encircles the building and a steel fence marks the boundaries of the site.

The building is equipped with the latest and most modern protective devices. The nearby

Back To Gold

Army Post provides additional protection. The Depository is equipped with its own emergency power plant, water system and other facilities. In the basement is a pistol range for use by the guards. The gold stored in the Depository is in the form of standard mint bars of almost pure gold or coin gold bars resulting from the melting of gold coins. These bars are about the size of an ordinary building brick, but are somewhat smaller. The approximate dimensions are 7 x 3-5/8 x 1-3/4 inches. The fine gold bars contain approximately 400 troy ounces of gold, worth $16,888.00 (based on the statutory price of $42.22 per ounce). The avoirdupois weight of the bars is about 27-1/2 pounds. They are stored in the vault compartments without wrappings. When the bars are handled, great care is exercised to avoid abrasion of the soft metal.

The Depository is headed by an Officer in Charge, who is responsible for ensuring the

Back To Gold

security of the gold. The guard force is composed of men selected from various Government agencies, or recruited from Civil Service registers. No visitors are permitted at the Depository. This policy was adopted when the Depository was established, and is strictly enforced. There are numerous conspiracy theories circulating around the Internet that the Gold contained within Fort Knox has spent. A delegation of Congresspersons in 1974 witnessed the gold first hand and reported of it.

Aerial picture of Fort Knox

Back To Gold

Executive Order 6102

Back To Gold

U.S. GOVERNMENT GOLD RESERVES
Current Report: June 30, 2016

Summary	Fine Troy Ounces	Book Value
Gold Bullion	258,641,878.074	$10,920,429,098.79
Gold Coins, Blanks, Miscellaneous	2,857,048.156	120,630,858.67
Total	**261,498,926.230**	**11,041,059,957.46**

Mint-Held Gold - Deep Storage

	Fine Troy Ounces	Book Value
Denver, CO	43,853,707.279	1,851,599,995.81
Fort Knox, KY	147,341,858.382	6,221,097,412.78
West Point, NY	54,067,331.379	2,282,841,677.17
Subtotal - Deep Storage Gold	245,262,897.040	10,355,539,085.76

Mint-Held Treasury Gold - Working Stock

	Fine Troy Ounces	Book Value
All locations - Coins, blanks, miscellaneous	2,783,218.656	117,513,614.74
Subtotal - Working Stock Gold	2,783,218.656	117,513,614.74
Grand Total - Mint-Held Gold	**248,046,115.696**	**10,473,052,700.50**

Back To Gold

**Federal
Reserve Bank-
Held Gold**

Gold Bullion:

Federal Reserve Banks - NY Vault	13,376,987.715	564,805,850.63
Federal Reserve Banks - display	1,993.319	84,162.40
Subtotal - Gold Bullion	13,378,981.034	564,890,013.03

Gold Coins:

Federal Reserve Banks - NY Vault	73,452.066	3,101,307.82
Federal Reserve Banks - display	377.434	15,936.11
Subtotal - Gold Coins	73,829.500	3,117,243.93
Total - Federal Reserve Bank- Held Gold	**13,452,810.534**	**568,007,256.96**
Total - U.S. Government Gold Reserve	**261,498,926.230**	**$11,041,059,957.46**

SOURCE: Fiscal.Treasury.Gov

Back To Gold

Book Value: The Department of the Treasury records U.S. Government owned gold reserve at the values stated in 31 USC § 5116-5117 (statutory rate) which is $42.2222 per Fine Troy Ounce of gold. The market value of the gold reserves based on the London Gold Fixing as of September 30, 2015 was $291.3 billion.

Deep Storage: That portion of the U.S.government-owned gold bullion reserve which the Mint secures in sealed vaults that are examined annually by the Treasury Department's Office of the Inspector General and consists primarily of gold bars.

Working Stock: That portion of the U.S. Government gold reserve which the Mint uses as the raw material for minting congressionally authorized coins and consists of bars, blanks, unsold coins and condemned coins. The gold

Back To Gold

reserve held by the Department of the Treasury is partially offset by a liability for gold certificates issued to the Federal Reserve Banks at the statutory rate, which Treasury may redeem at any time.

The Federal Reserve Bank building in New York, located at 33 Liberty Street in New York City, holds nearly 4 percent of the world's Gold reserves, amounting to 565 Billion US Dollars. It is believed that the Federal Reserve Bank building in New York has more Gold in it than Fort Knox, as it holds the Gold Bullion for over 38 nations on earth. The Federal Reserve Bank is a private corporation consisting of Banks but it has permission from the U.S. Department of Treasury to issue currency notes. There has not been any recent audit of the Gold Bullion held by the Federal Reserve Bank and the reasons for this have been stated as being too costly and expensive.

Back To Gold

DEEP SEA GOLD

Oil production companies have pioneered the technology to extract oil from the deep sea but now mining companies are taking advantage of the same technologies to extract gold. Nautilus Materials is one company that has pioneered the extraction of Gold in deep sea mining operations in the South Pacific. Deep Sea Mining is expensive, dangerous, and very lucrative. The world's oceans are known to contain 150,000 tons or more of extractable Gold. The United Nations International Seabed Authority oversees deep sea mining in international waters and will be issuing licenses to companies seeking to undertake these operations. Sustainable deep sea mining is a major concern as are environmental ones regarding the possible destruction of marine life habitats. The International Seabed Authority will maintain oversight on projects to prevent ecological disasters.

Back To Gold

GOLD MINING STOCKS

- Agnico Eagle Mines (NYSE:AEM)

- Asanko Gold Inc (NYSEMKT:AKG)

- AuRico Gold Inc (NYSE: AUQ)

- BHP Billiton Ltd. (NYSE: BBL)

- Coeur Mining Inc (NYSE:CDE)

- Comstock Mining Inc (NYSE: LODE)

- Gold Fields Limited (NYSE: GFI)

- Harmony Gold Mining Co. (NYSE:HMY)

- Highland Gold Mining Limited (LON: HGM)

- Nautilus Mineral (OTC: NUSMF)

- Nevsun Resources (TSE:NSU)

- New Gold (NYSE:NGD)

- Newmont Mining Corp. (NYSE: NEM)

- Real Gold Mining Limited (HKG: 0246)

- Seabridge Gold Inc (NYSE: SA)

- Shandong Gold Mining Co (SHA: 600547)

Note: Not to be construed as financial advice.

Back To Gold

GOLD BARS MANUFACTURERS

- Argor-Heraeus (Switzerland)
- Austrian Mint (Austria)
- Chin Hua Heng (Thailand)
- Credit Suisse (Switzerland)
- Degussa (Switzerland)
- Hang Seng Bank (China)
- Pamp Suisse (Switzerland)
- Perth Mint (Australia)
- Rand Refinery (South Africa)
- Tokuriki Honten (Japan)
- Valcambi (Switzerland)

These are just a sample of the companies available that make Gold Bars. There are many companies in many nations that make Gold Bars, but these companies mentioned here have a history and track record of successfully producing quality Gold Bars to international standards.

Back To Gold

GOLD IS LIQUID

Gold is a liquid asset but real estate is not. If you want to sell your real estate, you will have to hire a Real Estate broker and spend 1 percent or more of the value of the house, in order to sell it. Once it is sold, again you will have to spend money, this time for a sales commission and escrow fees. Before you are even paid, somewhere like 2 to 3 percent will have been shaved off your money. In addition, when you want to sell real estate, 3 months to 6 months is the average time that it will take for your home to sell. During an economic downturn, it has taken some individuals one year or more to sell their home, while financially struggling facing hardship. Real Estate is highly un-liquid and selling it is a long process that could test your nerves and make you wish that you bought Gold instead. Gold (bullion, coins, scrap gold) can be sold immediately after buying it with little or no loss whatsoever. Ornamental gold (jewelry) is not a

Back To Gold

South Dakota Gold Miners

great investment because you are likely to pay higher prices for the jewelry design itself and you will end up losing money when you sell it. But Gold Bullion, Gold Coins, and Scrap Gold can be melted down or sold in-tact. Items such as Gold Bullion, Gold Coins, etc should be purchased from professional Gold dealers that have a known and proven track record in the industry. You should not take risks (buyer beware!) when buying Gold. Because Gold is a liquid asset that can be sold as fast as you bought it, you should only buy Gold from

Back To Gold

trusted and ethical businesses. There is a reason why Central Banks own Gold and the reason is that it is liquid and can be sold in large quantities for not only money, but also for resources (oil, foods, etc.) My parent's home in Los Angeles took 2 years to sell during an economic downturn and the high costs that went in to selling it, left little or no profit remaining after taxes. I wish they had bought Gold instead.

Alaska Gold Miners

Back To Gold

GOLD TO PUBLISHING

The Homestake Mine in Lead, South Dakota, created one of the greatest sources of wealth known to mankind. George Hearst bought the Homestake mine for $70,000 and opened it in 1877. Up until 2001, this mine provided 10% of the total Gold that has ever been produced in the United States, making the Hearst Family immensely rich and powerful. Over 40 million ounces of Gold were produced from this mine in total and a large portion of its early Gold production was shipped to the Denver Mint, for refining. George Hearst's son William Randolph Hearst was an immensely influential figure that yielded great power and wealth through his near total control of newspapers and television. His father's Gold riches allowed William Randolph Hearst to purchase the San Francisco Chronicle in 1887 and build his business empire.

Back To Gold

FROM GOLD TO BOOKS

Anton Roman discovered Gold in Shasta City, California in 1851, making him a very rich man. He had undoubtedly witnessed the large amount of gold miners that found little or no Gold and decided that he should leave the Gold mining business. He sold his Gold, took the money, and created a small bookstore. His one bookstore went on to become 11 bookstores that are operating today known as Books Inc. Although Roman was not alive to see his bookstore go on to become a bookstore chain, the Gold that he discovered created and planted a seed that went on to sprout a fruit bearing tree. Roman, like Hearst, used Gold to venture in to other businesses that lived far on after their initial investments. Books Inc locations are in Northern California.

Back To Gold

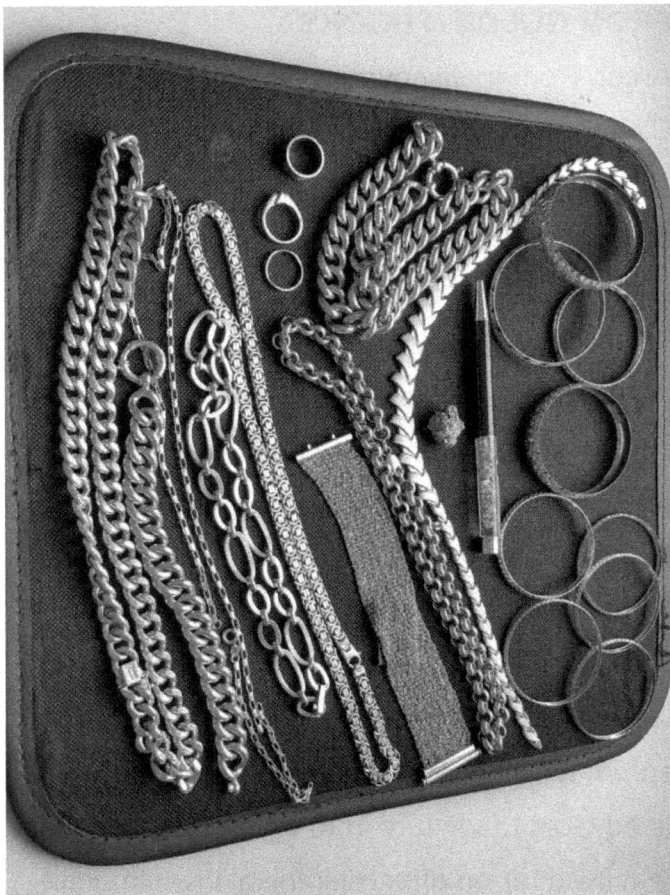

Gold Jewelry & Scrap Gold are melted in to Gold Bars

Back To Gold

Sutter's Mill

WHEN YOU SELL YOUR GOLD

Your gold is priced by the buyer based on the Karat value (6K, 10K, 14K, 18K, 22K, 24K) after it is tested. Then it is weighed and you are offered an amount based on the value. The selling value of Gold jewelry and Scrap Gold is always less than what you paid for it, unless you are referring to Investment Gold (Gold Bullions, Gold Bars, Gold Coins). When you purchase new Gold Jewelry or Scrap Gold (used Gold), you are essentially paying for the Gold with the addition of paying for the design

Back To Gold

and craftsmanship on the Gold. This is why when you choose to purchase gold, you should purchase Investment Gold rather than Gold Jewelry (unless you plan on wearing it!) or Scrap Gold. The price of Gold is a standard number that is listed publicly in newspapers, websites, and on economic TV shows. Research a few buyers before you approach them and seek the one that offers the most money for your jewelry or scrap gold.

Homestake Mine in Lead, SD (1900)

Back To Gold

AIRPORT GOLD

On November 26th, 1983 an armed gang carried out one of the one largest Gold Bullion heists of all time. According to BBC, they stole 76 boxes containing 6,800 Gold Bullion bars valued at over 30 million U.S. Dollars (worth over 300 million U.S. Dollars in 2016 value), on its way to the Far East. Dressed as Security Guards, they made their way in to the Brinks Mat warehouse in Heathrow storing the Gold and used physical force to get the alarm codes from the warehouse security. It is estimated that up to 15 people were involved in the robbery but only 3 were arrested. 2 of the 3 arrested received 25 years each in prison and 1 of the 3 received a lighter sentence of 14 years for handling the gold. The rest of the individuals involved in the robbery were never arrested and the majority of the Gold was never found.

Back To Gold

Gold Miner working on a rocker

Back To Gold

ARGUMENT FOR GOLD

Gold has certain advantages that real estate
can simply never possess:

1. Real Estate Takes Time To Sell

2. You have to pay commissions and
    escrow fees when you sell Real Estate.

3. If you rent out your Real Estate and a
    problem occurs (piping), you are
    responsible for it. Your Gold has no
    leaky pipes or angry renters for you to
    deal with.

4. Gold does not depreciate like an old
    home that needs re-modeling. With
    Gold, you are just buying Gold. When
    you buy a house, you may be buying a
    Money Pit (that needs more money fed
    in to for it to be standard and
    acceptable).

Back To Gold

The Native American population was greatly reduced by the arrival of the Gold mining industry

5. You can carry Gold in your hand and around your neck. You cannot carry real estate around with you.

Back To Gold

6. Central Banks choose Gold over Real Estate for investment purposes.

7. Gold is rare and the minable gold reserves on land will run out in 20 years.

8. It has been used as currency for thousands of years and its perception as being valuable is permanent.

9. You can spend a small piece of Gold to purchase something you need. You cannot spend a piece of your real estate to buy anything.

10. Gold has historically been purchased to offset (hedge) the threats created by international economic instability. Purchasing real estate will not offset any losses from dollar devaluation.

Back To Gold

11. Gold is rare and cannot be re-produced. Land can and has been re-produced as in re-claimed land (land that is below sea level and has been raised by pumps).

12. Gold has in many cases beat inflation while real estate has struggled with doing so.

Gold Bars stacked

Back To Gold

Goldstrike Mine in Nevada

13. Gold is easily convertible in to Silver, Platinum, Seeds, or Livestock.

Back To Gold

14. Gold is rare because it arrived on earth from space meteorites, and if you gathered all the mined Gold in the world, it would not fill up two Olympic sized swimming pools.

15. Gold prices are standardized regardless of what city or nation you are in. Gold prices are international prices, so that investors can feel comfortable purchasing it.

16. Gold, in small pieces or weights, can be given as a wedding gift or graduation gift. Real Estate is rarely ever given as a wedding gift.

17. Gold requires no maintenance. Real Estate requires maintenance so that it keeps its original state. Gold requires no

Back To Gold

upkeep for it to maintain its original state.

18. Gold can be rented out just like Real Estate with no depreciation whatsoever.

19. Gold can be sold for and used for electronics, medicine, jewelry, and various industries. In other words, Gold has many uses to many people, making it always sought after.

12.5 Kilo Gold Bar

Back To Gold

GROWING GOLD

The dream of the alchemists of the Middle Ages was the transmutation of base metals in to Gold. Alchemists were searching for the secret to create Gold and many charlatans and fraudsters claimed that they held secret for doing so. Many of the alchemists were able to convince potentates to give them large sums of Gold for months at a time for the supposed creation of Gold. Unfortunately for the potentates that gave Gold thinking they could make more Gold, no alchemist was able to do so successfully. Many con-artists like Cagliostro and others enriched their own pockets while carrying out these experiments. Using techniques created by modern science, gold can be artificially synthesized in a laboratory using a particle accelerator, but the cost of such a venture is too expensive for it to be feasible.

Back To Gold

UNITED STATES FEDERAL MINE SAFETY & HEALTH ACT 1977

- File or make a complaint of an alleged danger or safety or health violation to a Federal or State agency, a mine operator, an operator's agent or a miner's representative.
- Participate in proceedings under the Act such as: testifying, assisting, or participating in any proceeding instituted under the Act, or filing a complaint with the Federal Mine Safety and Health Review Commission.
- A medical evaluation or to be considered for transfer to another job location because of harmful physical agents and toxic substances. (For example: a coal miner has the right to a chest x-ray and physical examination for black lung disease [pneumoconiosis] and potential transfer to a less dusty position if the miner has a positive diagnosis.)
- Withdraw yourself from the mine for not having the required health and safety training.
- Refuse to work in unsafe or unhealthy conditions. NOTE: You must notify the operator of the condition and give them an opportunity to address the situation.
- Exercise any statutory rights afforded by the Act.

Back To Gold

These statutory rights are guaranteed to all miners by Federal law:

- Right to select a representative for safety and health purposes

- Right to refuse to work under conditions or practices believed to be unsafe, unhealthy, or illegal

- Right to report a suspected violation or danger to the operator, miner's representative, or MSHA without discrimination or reprisal

- Right to have a representative participate in a pre- and post-inspection conference

- Right to have a representative accompany an MSHA inspector during inspection without loss of pay ("walkaround" rights)

- Right to effective health and safety training

- Right to free Black Lung examinations and tests

- Right to protection from discrimination for exercising statutory rights

Back To Gold

GOLD GLOSSARY

Arbitrage – Taking advantage of differing prices of the same item in various markets to profit from the difference in price.

Assayer – A specialist that analyzes the content in metal.

AU – Symbol for Gold on Periodic Table of Elements

Bedrock – Solid rock that contains gold on its surface.

Bear Market – An economy whose trend is downward.

Boiler Room – Salesperson that using hard selling tactics to force you to buy.

Bull Market – An economy whose trend is upward.

Claim – Mineral rights to exploit land.

Claim Jumper – A thief that attempts to steal your mineral rights.

Excavation – Process of rock removal.

Federal Reserve Bank – Private U.S. corporation that sets monetary policy and has

Back To Gold

the right given by the U.S. Treasury to issue monetary currency.

Fiat Money – Paper money.

Fineness – Purity

Flour Gold – Fine floating gold.

Fool's Gold – Fake Gold also known as Pyrite.

Futures Contract – Agreement to purchase a commodity at a date in the future.

Geologist – A rock specialist that is able to analyze rock formations and make predictions as to the location of minerals.

Grade – Condition. Used for rating Gold coins.

Gold Standard – Monetary system based around Gold as the medium of exchange.

Good Delivery – Standard for shipping precious metals that must be adhered to in order for acceptance of delivery.

Gully – Small channel formed by water.

Igneous rocks - Formed when molten rock also known as magma, crystallizes and solidifies. They melt close to active plate boundaries and

Back To Gold

then they rise to the surface. Igneous rocks are either intrusive or extrusive.

Impermeable – Rock which water cannot pass through.

Inflation – The loss of value in your money and purchasing power parity caused by the printing of excess money by the government to pay for goods and services.

International Seabed Authority – United Nations body overseeing deep sea mining.

Intrinsic Value – The actual worth of the metal content based on weight.

Jewelry – Ornamental items made from precious metals and worn on the body.

Joint Venture – Agreement between Mineral Rights Owner (Patented or Un-Patented) and an operator to prospect and produce minerals.

Karat – Purity level of precious metal.

Kilograms – 1,000 grams.

Liquidity – The degree to which you are able to convert an asset in to cash.

Back To Gold

Lode Mining – Rock formation mining of minerals located in veins.

Magma - Molten rock. Magma could be completely liquid or a mixture of liquid rock, dissolved gases and crystals. Molten rock that flows to the surface is lava.

Mercury – Liquid metal used for Gold extraction.

Metamorphic Rock - A rock that's experienced chemical changes caused by the increase in heat or pressure.

Mine – Area of deep excavation for mineral extraction.

Miner – A person that produces minerals from alluvial or lode rock. The lowest paid profession in the United States.

Mineralization – Formation of new materials.

Moh's Scale of Hardness – Measurement of scratch resistance of various materials.

Nugget – Raw un-refined gold that can be picked up by fingers.

Numismatist – Coin Collector.

Back To Gold

Operator – Prospecting professional (individual or company) that specializes in mineral sourcing and extraction methods.

Ounce (Troy) - 31.1034768 grams

Patented Claim – Ownership of land and mineral rights to the land.

Placer Mining – Creek bank or river bank mining of alluvial deposits.
Premium – Paying extra for an item.

Prospecting – Searching for minerals to extract.

Quarry – Site for extraction of minerals.

Quartz – A common Gold bearing rock

Riffles – Ridges in the bottom of a sluice box that catch gold.

Scrap Gold – Used or second hand Gold.

Sedimentary - Sedimentary rocks are formed from pre-existing rock formed from deposits which have accumulated on the surface. Sedimentary rocks have layering.

Solid Gold – 24K Gold

Back To Gold

Stake – Marking the corners of a claim.

Ton (Metric) – 1,000 Kilograms

Trench - Trenches are deep linear zones that form where an oceanic plate sinks under another plate.

Un-Patented Claim – Ownership to the mineral rights of a land without actual property ownership.

Vein – Area that in rock formation that contains minerals for extraction.

Yield – Annual Return on Investment (ROI)

Back To Gold

U.S. BLM MINING LAW

Mining Law Administration

This includes the General Mining Law of 1872, as amended; those portions of the Federal Land Policy and Management Act of 1976, as amended (FLPMA) that affect the General Mining Law; and the Surface Resources Act of 1955. See the brochure Mining Claims and Sites on Federal Lands.

1. Mining Claim Recordation and the Annual Maintenance Fee

This program area, established by section 314 of the FLPMA (43 USC 1744 and 43 CFR 3833) and amended by annual budget acts, concerns the location and recording of mining claims and sites, recording of title transfers to mining claims and sites, payment of annual fees and filings of annual assessment work documents, and deferments of assessment work. It also includes the adjudication of these required filings, fees, and transfers, and the issuance of decisions voiding out claims and sites that fail to comply with these requirements. The Bureau has on record (1998) approximately 290,000 mining claims Nationwide, including Alaska. The BLM's annual statistics for mining claims are published in the Public Land Statistics.

2. Mineral Patents

The General Mining Law of 1872, as amended (30 USC 29 and 43 CFR 3860, provides the successful mining claimant the right to patent (acquire absolute title to the land) mining claims or sites if they meet the statutory requirements. To meet this requirement, the successful claimant must:

For mining claims, demonstrate a physical exposure of a valuable (commercial) mineral deposit (the discovery) as defined by meeting

Back To Gold

the Department's Prudent Man Rule(1)and Marketability Test(2)

For mill sites, show proper use or occupancy for uses to support a mining operation and be located on non-mineral land.

Have clear title to the mining claim (lode or placer) or mill site.

Have assessment work and/or maintenance fees current and performed at least $500 worth of improvements (not labor) for each claim (not required for mill sites).

Meet the requirements of the Department's regulations for mineral patenting as shown in the Code of Federal Regulations at 43 CFR 3861, 3862, 3863, and 3864.

Pay the required processing fees and purchase price for the land applied for.

The BLM administers this program through its 12 State Offices and the Headquarters office.

The program has two essential components, adjudication and mineral examination. A staff

Back To Gold

of land law examiners in each State Office adjudicates applications for completeness and compliance with the law and regulations. All aspects, except the mineral examination are handled here. Once the application has successfully passed through the adjudication process, the case is assigned to the BLM field office for a formal mineral examination to verify the discovery of a valuable (commercially viable) mineral deposit on the mining claims and proper use or occupancy for any mill sites. Mineral examiners are BLM geologists and mining engineers who have been certified by the Director to perform mineral examinations and to compile the necessary mineral report demonstrating the applicant's compliance with this aspect of the General Mining Law. Applications not demonstrating a discovery or proper use or occupation are subject to a mineral contest proceeding and possible loss of the associated mining claims and sites. If the

Back To Gold

mineral report confirms the discovery of a valuable mineral deposit and/or proper use and occupancy for any associated mill sites, BLM will send the application to the Secretary of the Interior for final review and action. If the applicant is successful on all points, BLM issues a mineral patent for the land applied for. Note: Since October 1, 1994, Congress has imposed a budget moratorium on BLM acceptance of any new mineral patent applications. Until the moratorium is lifted, the BLM will not accept any new applications.

3. Surface Management Program

This program area concerns authorizing and permitting of mineral exploration, mining, and reclamation actions on the public lands administered by BLM. It is mandated by section 302(b) of FLPMA (43 USC 1732[b] and 603[c]; 43 CFR 3802 and 43 CFR 3809). All operations of any nature that disturb the

Back To Gold

surface of the mining claim or site require authorization. The necessary authorizations and permits are obtained through the proper BLM field office.

The BLM regulations establish three levels of authorization, (1) casual use, (2) notice level, and (3) plans of operations. Casual use involves minor activity with hand tools, no explosives, and no mechanized earth moving equipment. No permit is required. Notice level activities involve use of explosives and/or earth moving equipment. The total annual unreclaimed surface disturbance must not exceed 5 acres per calendar year. A plan of operations is required for all other surface disturbance activities. A full environmental assessment and reclamation bonding are required.

Back To Gold

4. Surface Use and Occupancy

This program area concerns the proper occupation (residency or seasonal occupation of mining claims by mining claimants. It is administered pursuant to the Surface Resources Act of 1955 (30 USC 611-615; 43 CFR 3715). It provides that if you live on a mining claim or site, the occupation must be justified as reasonably incident to mining and exploration and that no other reasonable options for shelter are available while working the claims. The occupation must be authorized by the proper field office through a notice or plan of operations. There are severe penalties for unauthorized residences and occupancies (see the regulations at 43 CFR 3715).

5. Valid and Existing Rights Determinations

Holders of mining claims and sites located within lands later withdrawn from mineral entry must prove their right to continue to occupy

Back To Gold

and use the land for mining purposes. The owner must demonstrate they contain a discovery of a valuable mineral deposit and/or are used and occupied properly under the General Mining Law, as of the date of withdrawal and as of the date of the mineral examination. Mining claims or sites whose discovery or use or occupation cannot be demonstrated on the date of withdrawal or the date of mineral examination have no valid existing rights and will be contested by the Department.

1. The Prudent Man Rule was first defined in Castle v Womble, 19 LD 455 (1894), where the Secretary of the Interior held that: "Where minerals have been found and the evidence is of such a character that a person of ordinary prudence would be justified in the further expenditure of his labor and means, with a reasonable prospect of success, in developing

Back To Gold

a valuable mine, the requirements of the statute have been met."

2. The Marketability Test was first defined by the Secretary of the Interior in Solicitor's Opinion, 54 ID 294 (1933): "...a mineral locator or applicant, to justify his possession must show by reason of accessibility, bona fides in development, proximity to market, existence of present demand, and other factors, the deposit is of such value that it can be mined, removed, and disposed of at a profit."

Back To Gold

ACKNOWLEDGEMENTS

Bureau of Land Management (BLM)

National Park Service

United States Geological Survey

Shervin Khoramianpour

California State University Dominguez Hills

Toi Museum

Professor Annie Whetmore

Back To Gold

NOTES

Back To Gold

NOTES

Back To Gold

NOTES

Back To Gold

NOTES

Back To Gold

NOTES

Back To Gold

NOTES

Back To Gold

NOTES

Back To Gold

NOTES

Back To Gold

NOTES

Back To Gold

NOTES